PowerPhonics™

# In the City

## Learning the Soft C Sound

### Christine Figorito

The Rosen Publishing Group's
PowerKids Press™
New York

I pay fifty cents to ride the bus around the city.

I see cars and buses drive around the circle in the city.

5

I see people in the city.

I see cars in the city.

9

I see buildings in the city.

I see stores in the city.

I see a police officer in the city.

I see the center of the city.

I see the city park.

I see my friend Cindy in the city!

# Word List

center

cents

Cindy

circle

city

# Instructional Guide

**Note to Instructors:**
One of the essential skills that enable a young child to read is the ability to associate letter-sound symbols and blend these sounds to form words. Phonics instruction can teach children a system that will help them decode unfamiliar words and, in turn, enhance their word-recognition skills. We offer a phonics-based series of books that are easy to read and understand. Each book pairs words and pictures that reinforce specific phonetic sounds in a logical sequence. Topics are based on curriculum goals appropriate for early readers in the areas of science, social studies, and health.

**Letter/Sound:** **soft c** – Have the child name words with initial consonant **s**. List the words and have the child underline the initial **s** in each of them. Continue similarly with initial consonant **hard c** words (*cut, cold, cap, cake, cab, can, car*). List and pronounce the following words: *center, cider, cents, circle, city, cereal.* Lead the child to conclude that the words in the third list have the same beginning sound as the initial **s** words, but the same first letter as the initial **hard c** words. Identify them as words beginning with the **soft c** sound.

**Phonics Activities:** Have the child tell whether they hear **soft c** at the beginning or at the end of the following words: *dance, circus, ice, cereal, face, mice, lace, cell, cent.* As the child responds, list the words in two columns, according to the location of the **soft c**. Have the child underline the **soft c** in each of them.

- Have the child name **soft c** words to complete each of the following sentences: *For breakfast, I have toast and _____ (cereal). A round shape is a _____ (circle). A dime equals ten _____ (cents). A drink made from apple juice is called _____ (cider). A place where lots of people live and work is a _____ (city).*
- Have the child underline the **soft c** in each of the words from the above activity. Have them name the vowel that follows each **soft c**. Pronounce several words that begin with **hard c**. Have the child underline the **hard c** in each word and name the vowel that follows it. Lead them to conclude that **c** followed by **i** or **e** usually has a soft sound, while **c** followed by **a**, **o**, or **u** has a hard sound.

**Additional Resources:**
- Isadora, Rachel. *A City Seen from A to Z.* New York: HarperCollins Children's Books, 1992.
- Isadora, Rachel. *Listen to the City.* New York: The Putnam Publishing Group, 1999.
- Johnson, Stephen T. *Alphabet City.* New York: Viking Penguin, 1999.

Published in 2002 by The Rosen Publishing Group, Inc.
29 East 21st Street, New York, NY 10010

Book Design: Ron A. Churley

Photo Credits: Cover, pp. 13, 15, 19 © SuperStock; p. 3 © Omni Photo Communications, Inc./Index Stock; p. 5 by Haley Wilson; p. 7 © Richard Laird/ FPG International; p. 9 © David Bases/Index Stock; p. 11 © Todd Powell; p. 17 © Rudi Von Briel/Index Stock; p. 21 © International Stock Photo/Index Stock.

Library of Congress Cataloging-in-Publication Data

Figorito, Christine, 1971-
   In the city: learning the soft C sound / Christine Figorito.— 1st ed.
      p. cm. — (Power phonics/phonics for the real world)
   ISBN 0-8239-5918-X (lib. bdg.)
   ISBN 0-8239-8263-7 (pbk.)
   6-pack ISBN 0-8239-9231-4
1. Cities and towns—Juvenile literature. [1. Cities and towns.
2. City and town life.] I. Title. II. Series.
   HT152 .F54 2002
   307.76—dc21

                                        00-013107

Manufactured in the United States of America